# SNOW ON FIRE

## POETRY & NOTES

*Best Wishes to Elizabeth ♡ Roslyn*

### ROSLYN A. NELSON

SNOW ON FIRE

AUTHOR: ROSLYN A. NELSON

BOOK & COVER DESIGN: ROSLYN A. NELSON

Publisher: Little Big Bay
littlebigbay.com
ISBN: 978-0-9892822-6-0
Library of Congress Control Number: 2014916720

# TABLE OF CONTENTS

# INTRODUCTION

It was near the end of a day where nothing was really wrong ... or quite right. It had been productive, but too much detail work for this creative soul had set my brain on edge. I needed to be carried away, so I sat down with "Snow on Fire." Just two poems in, and the relief of connecting with Ros' world brought me to tears.

> "In my brain, solstice dawns
> slowly, as kindness might spread
> from touch, relegating
> convoluted and lonely landscapes
> of winter to distant memory."

See what I mean?

One stanza and my weariness melted toward hope, conjuring up images of a healing warmth spreading over a cold landscape – or was it my heart?

That's what Ros' writing does: it transports us and transforms our current setting into something deeper and sharper. It takes what she experiences in her gentle and wild small-town Wisconsin life and makes it feel intimately relatable. Wait – was it Ros who saw the deer prints and evidence of "disturbing feathered battles" on the snow as a short story, or did I? Was it Ros who confused a shirt's laundered scent with love, or did I? Was it Ros who wrote to Santa, who raged at the threat of an open pit mine, who pondered the ingredients in cat food, and who answered, once and for all, the question, "If a tree falls in a forest and no one is around to hear it, does it make a sound?" or did I?

Don't, however, mistake Ros' poetic sensitivity for a gooey softness or a calendar pitch. Just when I allow her words to sooth my soul with alluring imagery, she snaps my mind from reverie to reality, or shocks me with a burst of snort-out-loud wit doled out in poetic form (think Mary Oliver + Rilke + Annie Dillard):

> "Like picking up a magazine and finding
> that someone had filled out the quiz,
> 'How sexy are you?'
> and you know that person
> and you can never tell them that you also know
> their score."

Ros reminds us on each page that humans have a choice to remain disconnected from the landscape around and within them, or be relentlessly present.

May we all be aware enough to notice and care about the snow on fire.

*– Starla J. King, Writing Coach*
*and author of "Wide Awake. Every Day.*
*Daily Inspiration for Conscious Living"*

# SNOW

*In my life, I often choose wallpaper;*
*wallpaper removal vs. snowshoeing.*
*I'm not proud of this*
*but it seems like a good time to admit it.*
*Perhaps I can improve on this bad attitude in the*
*winter to come. Rumor is that it will be colder than*
*usual. Folks in Northern Wisconsin are hoping this*
*does not mean colder than last year's polar vortex.*

## Snow Warning

We took the last of the garden
inside in a hurry.
The forecast was for snow
and we didn't feel safe.

Later, beyond the window
out there in the dark
was that pitch night muffling to white?
Had we left anything in the garden?
Were the geraniums all in?

It was hard not to dream of ice
but, like most years, morning came
and there was no snow.
The wind blew a little harder.
The leaves were browner
but it had been a false alarm.
No snow.

Yesterday when I was busy
doing all this fearful work,
I heard the snort of deer, angry
that I had disturbed them. There were two.
And after that chastisement, they bolted
in true splendor, bounding away
navigating the trees effortlessly.

Once winter does arrive
it will narrow us to paths,
make choices for us,
force us to celebrate and tell stories.

Here's a story about the future.

Next year, I'll leave the garden gate open,
let those deer come in and finish off the parsley
and kale and chard.
Wander, without task, into the house.
Never think about the snow.
Watch them eat the garden.
Fall fearlessly asleep.
Navigate the snowless night.

Effortlessly.

## SNOW ON FIRE

A quiet morning in the forest,
the usual: soft, gray, white.

Quite lovely, wedding-mint green
lichen on the gray trunks.
And nearby, newly planted apple trees
secret with unrealized buds.

(Are the trees watching back?
Discussing my species, height
and unrealized potential?)

Through the snow, a flame
races up a white pine.
A red squirrel lit to orange with life
takes my breath away.

The sky opens to blue,
such a pale, delicate blue
that English china cups
are inspired
to shattering jealousy.

In my brain, solstice dawns
slowly, as kindness might spread
from touch, relegating
convoluted and lonely landscapes
of winter to distant memory.

It is a quiet morning in the forest,
the usual: soft, gray, white.
The straining sun and the powder blue.

The fearless squirrel running
up the cold tree.

Snow on fire.

## As White As Snow

In these short, polar days
I see blue in the bright snow
and imagine bear dens
warm and moist with breath.
But as the months wear on
it's no easy task to find a story.

So, I am prepared.
I have my clichés and like crazy quilts,
they were made for winter.

Pretty as a peach, I sit by
a babbling brook in the dappled shade,
Though yesterday held
not a glimmer of hope,
today I catch the sideways glances
which, even in this bone-chilling cold,
hold a key to my heart.
In the glorious sunset
or at the crack of dawn
and on nothing but a wing and a prayer
I wish upon a star,
look on the bright side

and count my blessings.

It's as clear as mud.

Be it ever so humble,

though cold as ice

in the dead of winter

there's no place like home.

## SNOW FALLING FOREVER

I tossed out an apple for the doe.
Her head tunneled into the snow
falling straight down, falling
all night now and still, very still
into the morning

of the world which is spinning
if you live in New York
at 700-900 miles per hour.
Falling into an atmosphere
which would continue to spin
around 1,000 miles per hour
if the earth were to stop.

Hold on to your hats
cats and computers
to the cows and your daily
bread and butter
which could end up on
someone else's toast, that is,
if the earth were to stop.

But the earth still spins,
snow still falls.

The doe's head comes up now
snowy nose and chewing
Galileo's apple, no doubt
which fell as fast as the snow
and did not fly off into deep
space, as it should at this speed.

Carefree and relentless.
Steady and quiet, the forest has filled
up to its knobby deer knees with snow.

Not tossed from the leaning tower
or spun from earth and lost in space.
Not landing by error, in yesterday
or tomorrow. Just falling forever today,
holding us to the ground.

This is what we said we wanted.
Some safety, and there it is.
One flake resting on the eyelash
of the doe, who stares
without blinking.

# A MILD WINTER

It wasn't a hard winter and for that,
we worried, so when the blizzard came and snow
sat down in the deck chairs, adding pillows to their
cold slats, we loved it.

We loved the inconvenience and cold necks and our shoulders
rose up to where they belonged, just below the ears.

We loved being snowed in and feeling timeless and safe
knowing that the neighbors and the town nearby
and the kids home from school all felt the same happiness.

How often do you know happiness?

The town plow came after two days.
It picked up my footprints
made when struggling to the road to see about the mail.
Scooped the v-shaped deer prints and enigmatic, disturbing
feathered battles written white on white.
Lifted all those short stories and piled them
on either side of the driveway where they melted
slowly into spring, found the river,
babbled frantically downhill, downhill.

My basement geraniums are straining to get out,
pressing leaves against the glass, hoping
to hear the departing tale,
paths and prints and battles, gone to sea.

# RECOGNITION

*"Looks like a great, grey morning directly ahead.
I heard a robin singing her praises.
I don't think I can top that so I'm going to
quiet down and listen."*

*– Mike Wiggins Jr. tribal member,
Bad River Band of Lake Superior Chippewa*

# Dear Santa,

I have everything I ever wanted.
Even when I feel deprived, this is true.

So, send my friends what they need this year:
Inspiration to the poets and artists;
a Sense of Awe to parents;
a Good Oven to the bakers;
Health to the activists;
Courage to defenders of the Earth.

May you hear the animals talk on Christmas Eve
and be flooded with gratitude for the mystery
and beauty of the world.

Look! We are alive at the same time!
There are no coincidences!

I am glad to be here with you. Merry Christmas.

– *Facebook Christmas greeting, 2011 & 2013*

## TWENTY

Solstice is near and an owl
sees everything that moves.
The deer graze so slowly
through the deep snow.

Coming in my direction.
I do not breathe.

A giant bird flies the path
of a red and white arrow
and crosses the road.

We are thinking of the
twenty children tonight.
A cradle hangs above the trees,
a milky, white, crescent moon
moist with clouds.

I know what I see and I see
the unrocked moon
which I cannot reach
to comfort.

*Remembering Sandy Hook Elementary School*
*December 14, 2012*

# MESSAGES

I love Google searches which think
for me. As I put in words spelled
badly, Google struggles to make sense
of my fingers on the wrong keys.
Without any judgement.

If I type in: Mary Oliver, it gives me Mary
Oliver who married James Lobb
in 1794 "after Banns at St Merryn"
when I really wanted to know
about a poem that might be
called Messages.

Haven't found it yet but I am sure
that Google will come through.

It has offered, in place of Messages,
Wild Geese, Thirst and Henry Carpenter
marrying two women
named Mary Polly, but unable to locate
Henry's wife Mary Oliver.

Ah! A few more clicks and success
is mine, where I find Messenger
not Messages and the first line
"My work is loving the world."

Something we all agree on.

Thank you Mary.

Thank you Google.

## DOUBLE NEGATIVE

Today is weeding, feeling the cold dirt.
Getting what might have been a love letter.
Reading the letter and finding
chalk-on-the-blackboard: "irregardless."
Feeling the spell break.

Today is keeping an eye out
pushing hair back to better see
the sweepstakes van, balloons and roses
just in case it's coming up the drive.
Then, looking down,
pushing hair back again to better see
rows of barely-sprouted early crops.

Looking up, looking down.

Reading the letter again, while stirring a pot.
Burning the letter, knowing another will not come.
"Irregardless."

Today is waiting for simple things:
unconditional love, a new car from Oprah,
peace and understanding,
a waistline and more hair.

Oh, and one more thing.
Eternal life.

The future carries a great burden.

I turn off the stove and turn off the lights.
The road is empty.

Meanwhile, baby rabbits listen to the bears
who dance all night in the clearing
and shake off their sad, winter fur.

Purposeful, falling stars thrill to feel
gravity embrace their cold bodies.
They sizzle into the lake.
The turtles are terrified and rush inside.
Loons dive to capture the five-pointed
feast of heat and otherworldliness.

This is what the world yearns to give me,
falls all over itself to lay at my feet.

But I scratch in the garden and wait
for life to drive up the driveway,
hand me a 3 x 5 foot check
and a hothouse rose.

# HATS OFF TO MY NEIGHBORS

To Poca who grows cabbage heads
collared by layered, leafy ruffs which
take up alarming square footage
in the precious, fertile soil.

Hats off to Kris and her 1,500,000 bees
in pastel hives beyond the driveway;
Kris, who might have an ailing bee
or two, tucked in a little bed in the house
covered with a black and yellow blanket
keeping a bee temperature of 95 degrees
until well enough to go back outside.
If this is true,
the children in the house
would take it for granted
and tiptoe past the sick room.

Kudos to Becky Brown who not only
has a melodious name but wanders
through her forest collecting seeds
and grows thousands of native plants,
elevating what we have failed to see
to its rightful state of glory.
She told me that she has
smelled bears. She has walked
through a cloud
of their huge scent.

Blue ribbons to Mike and Ellen
who moved from Los Angeles.
Now, in January when it rains ice,
they go to the barn and feel the bellies
of their horses to make sure
that they are warm.
I bet the horses like it too.
Adored horses called
Pork Chop and Sweet Pea.

And not lastly, give my warm regards
to the people I never
meet. Who live at the end
of long, dirt driveways.
I know that you are lifting
your wet baby from the bath
into the warm, dry towel.
And I know that you haven't
finished insulating or
drywalling or mudding or
building a fence around the garden
which you haven't dug yet.
But you are thrilled and know
that your new life together
will be perfect.

## One Hand Clapping

A tree fell in the forest.

I was not there.

I heard it.

So now that's settled.

# INTERSECTION

It was summer in the city,
warm without pity along the avenues
and no wind cooling the dark
red brick buildings sweating in displeasure
through humming window units.

We waited at the light.
A few steps behind him, I listened.
His raised hands animated the hot air
and he offered a flow of unintelligible words
and smiles, warmly enjoying conversation
with an unseen, good listener.

No one was there, on sidewalk or in windows.
Just me, off his radar, and poor competition
for his invisible sidewalk friend.

He felt like a nice man and the word "harmless"
came to mind. I continued to eavesdrop.
Halfway across the intersection, he paused,
quieted, and looking squarely at the light ...
at the glowing, green, walking man.
And finished his conversation
as the light changed to stop.

That's the poem I want to be.

## RIDGE LINE BIRD

In November rather late with the sun just so,
I stood looking out the kitchen window.
Before me lay the shadow of my house:
a gray layer over frost-weary grass, a translucent
chimney-topped windowless geometry
lengthening in a struggling sun.

If I had turned away too soon
from this silent reflection of my life,
I would not have seen a softer shape break
from its perch. Slender shadow legs lifted
from the pale ridge line and fluttered
to vanish as evaporated light in the winter sky.

A living shadow with hollow bones
gave itself to me while I stood barefoot, opaque
and chilly at the kitchen sink, my own form
a vertical sundial spike born to chase after time,
keep an eye on itself, and find some slippers.

With one small change.

On this November afternoon
in a single moment
beating wings rejoined the light
that had born them.

## HOW GOOD LOVE SMELLS

When I was fifteen
at the junior high school dance
swaying sort of dancing
shy and overcome
my nose was on the shoulder of a boy
on his very clean, pressed shirt
as I prayed not to step on his foot.

Oh, that springtime odor!
The smell of a young boy
as smelled by a young girl.

Inhaling and yearning.
I only realized years later
that I had fallen in love
with his mother's laundry.

## THE NEXT BOOTH

My friend was helping me hang pictures
but we didn't have the hooks we needed.
It was Sunday afternoon
and the hardware store was closed.
The junk store did not have any.
The grocery store did not have any.

So, screw it, we went to Maggies to eat lunch
where, in the off season, everyone is acquainted.

My friend said hello to Willy in the next booth.
I didn't know him.

Then we had a conversation
about the hooks, with the waitress,
in which the term
well hung got tossed about.

The conversation shifted, we got our meal.

Suddenly Willy was at our table.
He said he couldn't help overhearing us,
so he had gone home,
found what we needed in his garage
and handed picture hangers to us
all neat in a little baggie.

# HOW TO WRITE A POEM

Make an O sound
as in AstOnishment
and point to the growling
stomach
of your heart.

# FOUR FEET

*"If you talk to the animals, they will talk to you*
*and you will know each other.*
*If you do not talk to them, you will not know them*
*and what you do not know, you will fear.*
*What one fears, one destroys."*

– *Chief Dan George*

## Rescue Cat

I'm sitting up in bed
thinking about coffee.
Outside is windy September.

I could get up and gather wood
or pull drooping plants from the garden
but Miss Nimbus has chosen my lap
and snores like a Victorian lady.
Delicately.

So, I can't get out of bed.

I could clean the basement
and vacuum and put sheets on the guest bed.
The dishes are in the sink.
The laundry is wet.

But there's this business of the cat.

And god knows I haven't paid the bills
or washed the windows
where muddy bear prints
are enshrined from summer.
So much to do before winter.
Outside are chairs and a table

that should be inside.
And a rain barrel.
And a lawn mower.
And garden tools.
And geraniums.

What a shame
that I cannot do
any of these things.

There's this business of the cat.

## WHEN THE B͘     ͗T DIED

He was a cat everyone loved.
A retriever who loved to be vacuumed
and held like an infant child.
Before he died, his brother
curled up close and groomed him,
even with no response.

Still warm and soft, we buried him
with a bowl and some fresh grass,
something to throw up in the next life.
Such a little grave, dug that morning.
It did not seem right
to dig a grave for a living thing.

Now the light is long and gold and stretches,
cat-like, across the dew damp street and grass.
It matches the changing maples.
Wind blows. Birds land. Inside the house is stillness.

Everywhere I touch old places,
the flat white bedspread.
No, it does not answer.
The room where we held you as you died.
The pillow you slept on for those difficult last days.

The colored towel left next to it.
Is that dark shape my beloved friend?
No. It is nothing.

Nothing is everywhere in this house today.
Nothing is curled up on the chair.
Nothing meows to be taken outside.
Nothing wants breakfast.
Nothing is my dear, small friend.

In the back yard, I pick two apples from the tree.
The branch lifts without the weight.
One apple on your grave. A silly gift.
Cats don't eat apples.
One thrown hard across the street,
too far for you to bring back.

# AN EVENING WEDDING

The wedding guests sit down all at once.
There is a subdued swoosh,
as if they all wore taffeta undergarments.
As if a large vacuum seal had broken.
Their many daydreams resume.

The raccoon dreams too.
He has come up from the river
and pulls off his mask with that same swoosh,
with a cavalier toss.
It might have been a hat
tossed to the rack in the corner.

He can finally be himself, kick back,
expose his soul to the night sky and dark trees,
wash his hands of pretense.

The bride and groom turn to walk the aisle.
The guests wake up and rise.
This sound is a rustling one.
The raccoon goes home too,
dragging his little black mask;
he is not quite ready to go back to work.

But there is cake to be eaten.
Crayfish to catch.
There is that long, sleepless night.

# No Hurry

The porcupine chews salty wood
and a dog barks to be let in.
Already inside, the cat
slides a paw under the door
and samples the future.

Chewing, wagging, life moves along.
Doors open and close.
Some dogs are still barking.

Only the cat knows what's next.

And here's a lesson:
if life moves very slowly, don't pet it.

The porcupine moves like a snail.
If you have 30,000 quills,
you take your time.

I keep my hands to myself
go back inside the house
get on the floor with the cat
and see light through the crack.

# A TRUE STORY

Someone lost their dog
so I was looking, that night.
And – miracle – there it was,
trotting along the snowy road!
Pulled over quickly,
opened the door for the lost dog

and got a fox.

Drove on a little further,
pulled over again, to let out the fox
and got a coyote who was so mean
that when I saw the bear, I had second thoughts
but let him in too.

It was such a cold night. What else could I do?

In the back seat, fox, coyote and bear
sat side-by-side, perfectly behaved.
The ice on their fur melted and
all that breathing clouded the windows
while the heat lulled them to sleep.

I kept looking for the lost dog,
never found it and left the car door
open that night, a few inches,
so that when my companions woke
(having slept with the enemy),
they had an easy out.

The lost dog showed up
under a porch,
about two blocks from home.

I spent an hour getting the fur
off the back seat.
I should have left it there,
because when people hear this story
they never believe it.

## DOING WELL WITHOUT US

One day, the deer didn't move.

Their camouflage turned them

into trees and snow.

Accomplishing what we want,

they became part of the world

while we looked out the window,

circled the house,

searched for the door.


When the lake freezes

it does not reflect the sky or you.

Its view turns with each degree

of temperature and faces down

through itself, to the sandy bottom.

The sky is at its back

and we can walk

to the island.

It is easy to see the gray squirrel

on the gray tree and the brown deer

on the brown ground

the bubble of air

staring up from the ice

but it is not our sight that animates

the world.

## BREECH BIRTH OF SIGHT

At the top of the ridge walk three
sun-brightened deer, living also
in the upside down globe of my eyes;
eyes which flip the world on its head
and deliver deer and everything else
to my exhausted brain with delicate hooves
and high heeled shoes waving in the air.

At breathtaking speed, the images
pop right-side-up. Wheels get traction.
Deer keep their footing. Smoke rises.

I try not to think about it.
I press my feet to the ground.
A sun shower of rain
falls gratefully down and the startled crows
fly gratefully up. There is dirt on my shoes.
My brain keeps me on my feet
so that I can
save the world.

# SPRING

*I arrived home to two days of artificial spring which*
*would soon be followed by weeks of damp chill and*
*gray sky. But today was sunny, the sky was blue,*
*and we stopped in Iron River, or was it Brule? The*
*waitress was confidence itself and announced that*
*soup-of-the-day was Tomato Mac. Other clues that*
*we were now in Wisconsin were light fixtures made*
*of deer antlers; floor, walls and ceiling of highly*
*varnished wood; and when we ordered turkey, mashed*
*potatoes, and gravy, the bread was whiter than snow.*

# FALLEN TREE

When trees die
their trunks stand still for a long time.
Woodpeckers and insects feast on them
until the day they topple.
I don't know anyone who has seen them fall
but we all imagine the noise we didn't hear.

And leaves. They fall too and release an unbound book –
poems of sun and wind undone,
red and yellow stories of autumn lost and lowered
to an earth which conceals every word,
saves the crash and brittle losses
under white, quiet, perfect snow.

This is the work of the earth.

Come spring,
every tiny, green thing in the wet ground
will know its beginning.

## SPRING

The North has become tropical.
Again. Everything is beautiful.
Awash in ticks and gnats,
mosquitoes and biting flies.
Still beautiful.

The water in the cat's bowl
so pure and cool and golden
and in the evening, that cat
leans its muscled neck
against my mouth
so that I cannot see what I want to see
which is the less of me she wants,
less human and more her.

A simple day with sunlight.
Everywhere. Some gnats.
A clean house. Some animals.
Frogs crying Spring! Spring! Spring!

# THAW

Today I am so brave.

I will go out and meet
the earth, follow
the warm pattern of light across
the white forest floor, careful not to step
on shadows that crisscross
the back of mother spring.

What is ever green is breathing
ever tenderly, lifting and falling.
And the shadows breathe too.
I have seen a single tall plant
sway like this, independent of wind,
waved as if someone were hiding in the grasses
whose only job was to announce
the location of one splendid, milky green stem.

Soon there will be a roar.
Birch trees will top themselves
in green explosions.
The dense mass of summer wind
will arrive in the clearing with the power
of a million animated leaves behind it.
Stars will stop staring,
find their voices, and arrange
themselves into Constellation Summer.

Everyone can feel it coming.
Today you turn to the window
and wonder what has caught
your eye.

It is the breath of spring.
The people in their city beds and
the bears in their dens
moan in their sleep
because of it.

# PRIMAVERA

The light forced time to penetrate
itself and seasons too, folded
into gray, commanding
shivering surrender
with no choice but to follow

spring who crouches beyond the flat sky
of November's cool stare
and does not exhale,
does not expose her safe place
by fogging her captor's glassy eye.

Without a sound, she plans revenge.
Her April winds will bring
the spring flood,
the sea which rises in you.

We barely hear
the soft foot of spring
and carelessly inhale
the same air that lifts wings.

## ALMOST SPRING

The grass isn't green yet but high

in the blue sky

tree tops search for food

and squint-white clouds

in color-burning-out light

hover in brilliance.

It is not spring but the secret is out

and the snow that falls now

is from the branches.

## How Sexy Are You?

We hoped for the melt but it was too sudden.
The forest yielding its cover of snow
took us by surprise and we were unwilling
voyeurs of exposed, fallen limbs
and defenseless patches of wet earth.

Like picking up a magazine and finding
that someone had filled out the quiz,
"How sexy are you?"
and you know that person
and you can never tell them that you also know
their score.
So we hoped again, this time for spring
to hurry, to rush in with leaves
and cover it all back up again,
to ease our discomfort.

Nightfall offered a softer view.
One lamp in the front room spilled
generous pools of light outside
which for some hours dressed
the bare earth and trees
and let the forest
appear hushed and secure
the way it was before.

But the deer, beyond the light
pick their way on muddy ground.
They search for footing
with cautious, slender legs
and each step is courage.
They will find spring
even in the dark,
step by step.

## GERANIUM ZEN

Like the rest of the nation, we have had hot
weather for the past few days in Northern
Wisconsin – excepting a belt of lower temperatures
that ring the shores of Lake Superior.

But we got a break yesterday. Cool air finally
arrived and some rain fell last night – all of which
made this morning one of those which convinces
me that I live in the best place in the world.

I took my coffee and toast and sat outside on the
still-damp steps where it was quiet enough to hear
the sounds of the forest. I started, gradually,
to focus on tiny drops of rain still trapped in the
grass, reflecting light; the butterfly in the distant
green woods; the woodpecker's work; and the
growing plants. And, in the green foliage, I could
see the inquisitive silhouette of a favorite black bear
watching me back. It was truly a morning for which
to be thankful.

One of my potted geraniums, which had been
in the basement all winter, had grown only in the
direction of the window, long, bald stems straining
to be nearer the sun. I felt a little guilt over my
neglect, when I moved the gangly plant outside
in the spring. Now, thriving in full sunlight, small

leaves are sprouting on the scrawny side of the plant, self-correcting its lack of balance.

We are like that, I thought. If no one 'turns us during our winters,' we lose our balance and grow lopsided. I thought of all that I learn from my friends, even on the days when I resist.

It's a good day to remember the people who "turn you to the sun."

## TWO LOST DAYS

Two winter days got lost.
No one noticed until mid April
and then, of course, they had to be
inserted back into the calendar
before something awful happened,
Daylight Lost Time, for example,
or the abrupt addition
of two snow days in August.

I am watching the second
of these two days rage
outside the window.
Tall trees sway in circles
whipping the upper atmosphere.
Wind roaring a single, dark note.

These days have come to say,
"Don't forget who runs this show."

The second lost day is losing light.
Lowering the shade without promise
that April will return to normal,
tomorrow, and be warm.

No wonder that young animals
are afraid of storms,
coming to time with no memory of time.
Why should they believe
that a storm would ever end?
Why do I?
Somewhere in me, the young animal
thinks, "This might be the one
that doesn't turn toward spring.
This might be *that* lost day."

# METAL

*"Someday the earth will weep,*
*she will beg for her life,*
*she will cry with tears of blood.*
*You will make a choice: if you will help her*
*or let her die, and when she dies,*
*you too will die."*

– John Hollow Horn, Oglala Lakota

# Getting Yelled At

The deity Mercury had two children;
invisible household gods
who played with us
on that outstanding day
when a thermometer broke,
a bonus almost as sweet
as a snow day.

First, a scurry to recover the beads
where they trembled on the floor,
shimmering on uneasy axis.

Then, rolling in our hands,
we saw that mercury
liked being a sphere
and kept on being one.
In fact, the largest sphere grew,
absorbing the smaller ones
with no effort at all.

We did this until we got bored.
No one yelled at us to stop.

Now I am such a powerful
grown up that I can create mercury.
I just turn on the dryer
and heat my sheets with coal.

The silvery fish in the Sioux River
have it on their menu too.
Thanks to me,
the powerful grown up

And still, no one yells at me.

On days when spring
shines on the far end of the road
I wonder if someday
my whole world will be
aglow with silvery reflection
and it will be the only thing
that moves.

## METALLIC STAR

Today, a very brief star falls
back to its source.
Formed from earth and shot
into space, it now burns to death
without shriek or yell
at coming home to mother
at becoming light
in its reverse birthing.

Earth receives the sad star.

Opens to comfort.
Closes around.

Her diminished creation.

## OPEN PIT MINE

When the pit is done, and abandoned
the people will no longer think
clearly because their grief will have become
greater than any other sensibility.

They will gather rusted fragments
of metallic debris and haul them
to the edge of the pit.

Without ceremony, prayer or drum
the outdoor grills, cell phones and cars
will tumble to the lowest ledges,
some resting in shallow water.

Then the people will wait, to see
if these bits will serve as seeds and grow
back the watershed, the mountain's spine,
eagle, bear, healing plant and water.

It is very quiet here, by the pit
where they wait.

# Fired

When God landed a job at the mine, he was
thrilled, as he thought he had no relevant skills,
having been in management most of his life.

He was put in charge of overburden, so he spent
his first days at work digging graves. He buried
eagles, bears, porcupines, trout, deer, badgers, fisher,
crawfish, snakes, ferns, frogs, turtles, and trees. It
was hard on him; he remembered creation.
He remembered the first tight curl of the fiddlehead
fern and the first shrill voice of a newborn cub;
schools of tadpoles and translucent fish eggs.
No one else in the world remembered the first times
of everything, so his burden was a lonely one. People
noticed that he kept to himself.

The strain proved too great. He had trouble sleeping
and cried easily, but had no coverage for mental
health, so they moved him to the wetlands division.
The company would have preferred to fire him then
and there but they were worried that the press might
take an interest and the investors hated bad press.
The division was all but inactive. The company
had said from the beginning that they could create
wetlands but in truth, it was no job for mortals,
so perhaps this was a perfect match.

No one knew wetlands like God and he excelled at his new position but in no time at all, the depression returned, and that's when they finally got rid of him. There were no references and no severance pay; they just showed him the door.

Things were not looking good, so on that hot, August day, he caught a ride into Mellen and ordered coffee at the Snow Creek Cafe. The place was all but empty. Every so often, the noise of blasting broke the silence.

God lifted his coffee cup and smiled at the waitress. She smiled back. He was a good tipper.

He wondered what had gone wrong, how he had become so lost, and most distressing, he wondered who would forgive him.

Outside, three boys were wishing for something better to do than kicking rocks in the street. They decided to go to the river and on their way, walked right past the window of the Snow Creek Cafe where God sat, looking out at them. To their young eyes, he was just another sad, old man.

And that's exactly how God felt, on that day he got fired: sad, old, and human.

## VERY SHORT STORIES

*The sun had just set and the river ice was thin with*
*a few tracks and shifting air bubbles below.*
*I wondered for a moment if there was a mechanical*
*pump making all the water-in-motion sounds.*
*So noisy for a quiet, snowed-over place, the speed*
*of the water was thrilling, hidden under this placid,*
*white surface. On the way home, I saw that many tree*
*trunks looked velvet black. Not darkness or shadow*
*but something sooty that had come with the night.*

# SOMEONE ELSE'S MEMORIES

We are visiting relatives in Canada where my
mother grew up. I am ten years old. There's
a dog who sleeps in the kitchen under the table,
back legs contracting. He yips out ecstatic dreams
of himself catching food dropped by careless people
who love him wildly and toss every other forkful
on the floor. He twitches and moans, "I am alive!
I am alive!"

I am with kind people who do not wake him.

Still shy, at that same dream table listening to my
mother and her cousin, I am aware of a large, gray
coffee pot always hot, which sits on the stove. "In
the States" we percolate coffee. This cloth bag full
of grounds is a great mystery to me and the endless
pot holds the status of a religious icon. They "catch
up on the relatives" and show pictures of people
who I don't know but am somehow bound up with.

*Years later my mother's cousin will die of cancer
and before she does, she will tell my mother, a nurse
who knows about dying, "I'm a tough Icelander. This
won't kill me." But it will.*

My mother's cousin is good to me. There are no

other children around. I am grateful not to be pushed into happy relationship with strangers who have only their age in common. She tells me about the playhouse in the yard where I go and enjoy myself in quiet, sensing someone else's memories in the heat of the day and the stillness of the air. I play there with contented pleasure, as I do not yet differentiate between the past and the present.

"You can sleep in Kalli's room." We walk up a staircase with a heavily textured ceiling above us that twinkles. There is glitter in the plaster. I wondered what they were covering up. Someone's son has become a plasterer. It was awful, a crime against the house; I was so wise at ten. I knew what was being lost. If my mother were alive now, she would be amazed that I remember the plaster. She was always amazed that any part of her life was important to me. Who did she think I was?

Kalli was my grandfather and he was dead, so I am not sure I want to sleep in his room but am too shy to resist a grown up and figure that I can stay awake long enough to keep vigil and be safe until even the ghosts fall asleep. What do they talk about when

I am upstairs? Is that when they tell about the men who drink too much and women with daughters who have come to no good?

I am drifting asleep. Gratefully, the sheets seem not to smell of death but have a cool humidity in them. I heard that this house nearly floated away in the spring flood, but it seems okay to me and I am nervous that my relatives might not be very smart if they put the house right back in the same place where surely it will flood again.

When the dog wakes up he will stretch forward, straightening his front legs and rise to sniff out a meal. That's what I'll do too. I'm never the first one up and I hate entering into the kitchen to cheerful good mornings when I am still in a dream state and want to be invisible. Once that's over, I can blend back into the dream table and play with the sugar cubes and suck a little of someone's coffee through one. I can have toast and jam and milk and juice, whatever I want.

I am the child, the blessing.

We take our turns dying and holding on. The year my mother dies, I discover that I look just like her. I discover that she gave me everything to remember and nothing to hold on to. I take her ashes to

Iceland and bury them and get ashes and dirt all
over my hands and then later, I feel anguish that
I left her in such a lonely place, feeling that
I should race back and get her and make everything
warm again. I feel badly about that and wish
someone would convince me otherwise.

All these years later, and I am still ten years old.

# NOTES

When I first moved to town, it was not unusual for
two drivers to stop, window-to-window, anywhere
on the road, and talk. They appeared to be entirely
oblivious to anyone behind them and those of us
who were, just politely maneuvered around them.
Never was there a horn sounded. Never. Never.
It would have been rude.

I don't notice this happening much anymore but
if you call someone and get the wrong number, you
can have a nice conversation anyway. Pretty soon
you find out that the wrong number lives only
a couple miles away, is afraid of bears and thinks
she has met you somewhere.

One evening however, I got a call from someone
who wanted to spread sewage on my land. It took
me by surprise. We didn't have much of a conver-
sation but I later regretted that.

## Notes About Goldfish

Does that huge, golden carp in the restaurant tank
who dives down after a sinking morsel of food think
that he is heading to the ocean bottom?

Does he think that the light above where fluorescent
fixtures glimmer wetly at him is the great, limitless
sky and burning sun above the sea?

Are the giant human faces that peer at him visions of god?

Does the tiny ceramic mermaid drowning at the bottom
of his tank still haunt him, though he has outgrown her?

And when the fish (perhaps done secretly at night so as
not to disturb the patrons?) is scooped up with a net and
released from his endless and increasingly tight turnings
in the tank, does he gasp for air, or for water, or out of
grief that the end of the world is a Chinese restaurant?

## Dirty Words

I am usually caught by surprise when a word
changes status and becomes a DIRTY WORD.
These shifts occur spontaneously – even before
social media existed to accomplish rapid, group
think. One day, you're having coffee with friends
and say, for example, "actress" and it becomes clear
to you that "actor" is now The Word To Use.

Using "actress" can be overlooked, but beware
of these social faux pas: oriental, janitor, waitress,
garbage man and stewardess.

Oriental is one of my favorite words. Is it a dirty
word because it is thought to categorize a group
of people unfairly? I've never thought of it that way.
I see exotic and beautiful images in my mind's eye,
when I let "oriental" fall from my lips, albeit now
only whispered in private.

And what about "garbage man?" The term evokes
calloused hands, sweat-stained shirts, biceps, the
swing of the trash can, the confidence of physical
labor. When I hear "sanitation director" I see
a robotic form at a computer console. Trash
collector isn't much better.

The aversion to janitor, waitress, and garbage man all seem to stem from a profound discomfort around the labors of serving, cleaning, repairing and the like. What are we ashamed of? I've been a waitress and never needed to see myself as a "server," and as "waiter" was available for the men and boys, why did we need a unisex word to replace these?

Are you old enough to remember "having a janitor?" Janitors were iconic. Every school had a janitor, someone with personality! Someone who knew how boilers worked and kept the bones and muscles of the building humming reliably in the background of grade school education. Those were the days!

So, words change but I would like to suggest that too much sanitizing is not good for us and can even be dangerous. Words that people hide behind can damage us. Try "derivatives" on for size. Need I say more?

On a recent 2+ hour flight, I was seated next to a seven-year-old boy who was traveling alone. Romen was active, smart, verbal, and friendly.

He talked incessantly. He also shared his licorice and potato chips. I answered questions about planes crashing, why it felt bumpy, why he would not mind if we crashed over water (he had goggles in his backpack), and what to do when his ears hurt on descent.

He encouraged me to help him pulverize a baggie of cocoa puffs so that he could stick his finger into the cocoa 'powder' and lick it clean and he wanted to teach me how to play the video games on my phone. I was sad when I stood up to say goodbye and I saw, looking down at him, that his buoyant confidence had drained away.

He had been told not to leave his seat until an adult came to help him. Small and fearful, he looked up at me and asked, "Are you my stewardess?"

Ahhh ... if only.

## NOTES

Why isn't cat food made of mice?

# TARANTULAS IN BANANAS
HOW A CONVERSATION ON FACEBOOK MOVES FROM
SPIDERS TO VANILLA MALTS

**RN:** When you were a kid, did someone tell you that there might be tarantulas in bananas?

**TW:** Yes, yes! My grandparents and parents shopped at Anderson's Grocery in Northeast Minneapolis when I was in grade school. You handed them the list and they fetched everything for you using a hook on a long handle to knock down cereal boxes on high shelves. Those were the days when you bought groceries at one store, meat at the butcher shop and baked goods at the bakery. In a square candy case in the middle of the store they had a tarantula on display for quite awhile that came in a load of bananas.

**AK:** I'm not even going to look at the bananas I bought today.

**TG:** Yes, true. And snakes. Snakes in furniture too.

**TW:** How about a snake coming out of the vent in your car while you're driving?

**LW:** They found one at the local IGA but in grapes.

**NV:** They told us all kinds of crap back then. Remember duck and cover drills in the school hallways? Or giant white alligators in the New York sewers?

**BR:** Sally and I have an uncle who worked in a fruit market; he told me that there were often tarantulas in banana bunches. Doubt that it's true any more, having seen a banana packing operation in Costa Rica.

**RN:** I thought this tarantula things was a myth. Now I know better! And *white* alligators?

**BR:** It's an old myth. The bananas I saw were bagged while still on the tree, then washed, disinfected, and re-bagged in grocery-store-size bunches for shipping.

**TW:** Well, Bill, probably not true anymore but I do remember that big hairy thing in the candy case, probably around the late 1950s.

**CF:** A kid would never forget seeing a tarantula in a candy case. Never!

**TG:** I had a little van set up to do ski service work, would run around from department store to department store and mount bindings. Dayton's department store was one of my accounts. When I got to the loading dock one day there was a pest control guys with a big (4-5 square feet) sticky sheet. The furniture floor was closed and they were on there way to catch a snake. The flipped-out sales lady said it looked right at her, crawled out of the divan and disappeared behind the carpets.

**PS** My brother and I kept a tarantula for a pet. They are very affectionate.

**TW:** Ted, you're proving my theory that everyone who lived in Minneapolis back then worked for Dayton's at one time or another.

**NC:** Well, the spider in the bananas warning is actually valid. It's not always a tarantula, though. As a matter of fact, there's a tiny yellow spider that lives exclusively in banana trees and is highly venomous.

**RN:** Terry, one of my long-held theories is that everyone at one time or another has lived or will live in South Minneapolis. P.S. I worked for Dayton's.

**TW:** I knew it! And I wish it was still Dayton's. What neighborhood in South Minneapolis are you from? I'm a Nordeaster; I just married into South Minneapolis.

**RN:** Terry: the art school neighborhood near the Black Forest Inn, and later, 33rd and Dupont. Yes, I miss Dayton's. Remember the gallery? That store was an institution. As a first year art student, new to the Big City (Foshay Tower was the tallest building), I took a credit card given to me by my parents for emergency use only, and went to Dayton's for a vanilla malt.

# STUCK

*I worry about ridiculous things: the ermine whose coat*
*changed to white before the snow fell; the dinosaur*
*eggs that never hatched; or if I left the bath water*
*running when I left the house.*
*I read an online ad for cookie cutters which read:*
*"I have oak leaves, maple leaves, a butterfly,*
*Christmas tree, a pig, and a star.*
*I want what I don't have."*
*Here we are, stuck in the middle of god.*

## FIREFLIES

Sound asleep but instinct
woke me up
told me to look outside
stumble in the dark house,
dark door, dark doorway.
Open and peer into the dark night.
No moon.

Cold feet and eyes coming to life.

And there they were, the fireflies
who woke me up and let me see
their passionate code.
Making love in the dark sky
forming impulsive constellations.
Shaping light to yearning.

Other things glow in the dark
but no others tempt the stars
to fall from the sky
fall in love with mortals
and live on the warm earth.

## Saved by The Dark

I saw a bright light at the end of a tunnel.

It went out.

# DRIVE BY NOTES

AT THE SPEED OF LIGHT, THE LAKES GO BY,
COOL AND PRETTY.

There was a little body of fur in the middle of the road
and a fresh, white stripe of paint drew up, across, and
down that body, and continued on interrupting itself
as far as I could see.

CATTAILS BELLY UP TO THE DITCH
AND DRINK TO GET HIGH.

I read a story about a man who upped the voltage in his
keep-out-the-dogs fence so that it would really hurt.
The man fell into the fence and died. So, there was some
good news today.

MONET PADDLES AROUND,
WAVING BRUSHES AT THE LILY PADS.

The lady at the rest stop café must have spilled Shalimar
this morning or else believe that she is invisible and
needs a smell charm to keep other people from walking
through her.

HAY SOMERSAULTS INTO JELLY ROLLS.

A woman was picked up in the middle of the ocean.
She said she was in transition, becoming a sea-dwelling
person and had been living in the ocean for three days.
She wouldn't tell her name and was dressed in beige
slacks, a brown shirt and sneakers. The Coast Guard
forced her to come aboard.

AND A WHITE LAMB LEAPS AMONG
THE GRAY SHEEP.

## Lower Case G

God has been a proper noun long enough.

The real fall is not capitalizing
Dirt or Apple,
Asparagus or Wine.
Child or Dog.
Sunlight or Hearth.

Here's a petition for the Earth.
(There's a word we got right.)

Sign here to:
lower case eden and
upper case Compost,
lower case christmas and
upper case Love,
lower case buddha and
upper case Bear.

Sign here and commit
the sacrilege of tumbling from
grace into the puddles and ditches
of creation.

# PRETEND THAT I AM DEAD

for someday soon
if not already
it will be true and you
will own the world and remember
me as a name or echo
or more than likely

not at all.

For all your lack of regard
I still must deliver the world to you,
wishing you well
through gritted teeth.
Handing over the reins
of this rattling wagon
whose wheels scatter muddy earth
with each upward
release
and whose driver squints
at the diminishing sun
still in view.

For all of this,
which looks like loss,
imagine comfort.

Once scattered
we might find ourselves
airborne
and drift to earth
like seeds
that settle
for hope.

## ABOUT THE AUTHOR

Roslyn Nelson, author of *Snow on Fire,* lives near Lake Superior in a very small Wisconsin town where she is renovating a 100+ year old storefront for her graphic design (*glacialdrift.com*) and book design activities (*littlebigbay.com*) and for life-in-general.

Mellen, Wisconsin is at the foothills of an ancient mountain range, now worn to gentle hills called the Penokee Range. Under attack by a mining company, protection of this pristine watershed has been an important focus in her life in recent years. From the top of the ridge, pure bone-chilling water bubbles to the surface from totally uncharted sources and flows into Lake Superior – into 10% of all the fresh surface water in the world. A proposed open pit taconite mine would gut the streams and forests of the Penokee Range, destroy the priceless clean water, and pollute the area for the foreseeable future.

Her first book of poetry is *Raving About Summer ~ Fussing About Winter* and celebrates life in another small town: Bayfield, Wisconsin.

*Snow on Fire* is available on Amazon.com and other online book retailers worldwide.

Contact the author at www.littlebigbay.com.